*A late 19th century view of the north front of the house, showing the tall Victorian water tower on the left hand side. The tower appears to be twice its present height. The lion plaque seen today on the tower was added in the late 1960s. It came from Northwick Park, Gloucestershire, and is made of Coade stone, inscribed CROGGON 1833.*

# Welcome to Parham

Parham has always been a well-loved home, and only three families have lived here since its foundation stone was laid in 1577. The Hon. Clive Pearson, my great-grandfather, bought the House and Estate in 1922. He and his wife Alicia found it in sad repair, and together they revived and restored Parham with great sensitivity and care, collecting many interesting and beautiful things with which to furnish it. They opened Parham to visitors in 1948, not because they needed to, but simply because they wanted to share it with others. Their daughter Veronica Tritton, my great-aunt, followed them in this tradition. I have lived here with my family since 1993, and Parham is now owned by a Charitable Trust.

Parham's beauty and peace have changed little over the centuries, and it is still a very special place. I very much hope that you enjoy your time here.

Emma Barnard

Lady Emma Barnard

# CONTENTS

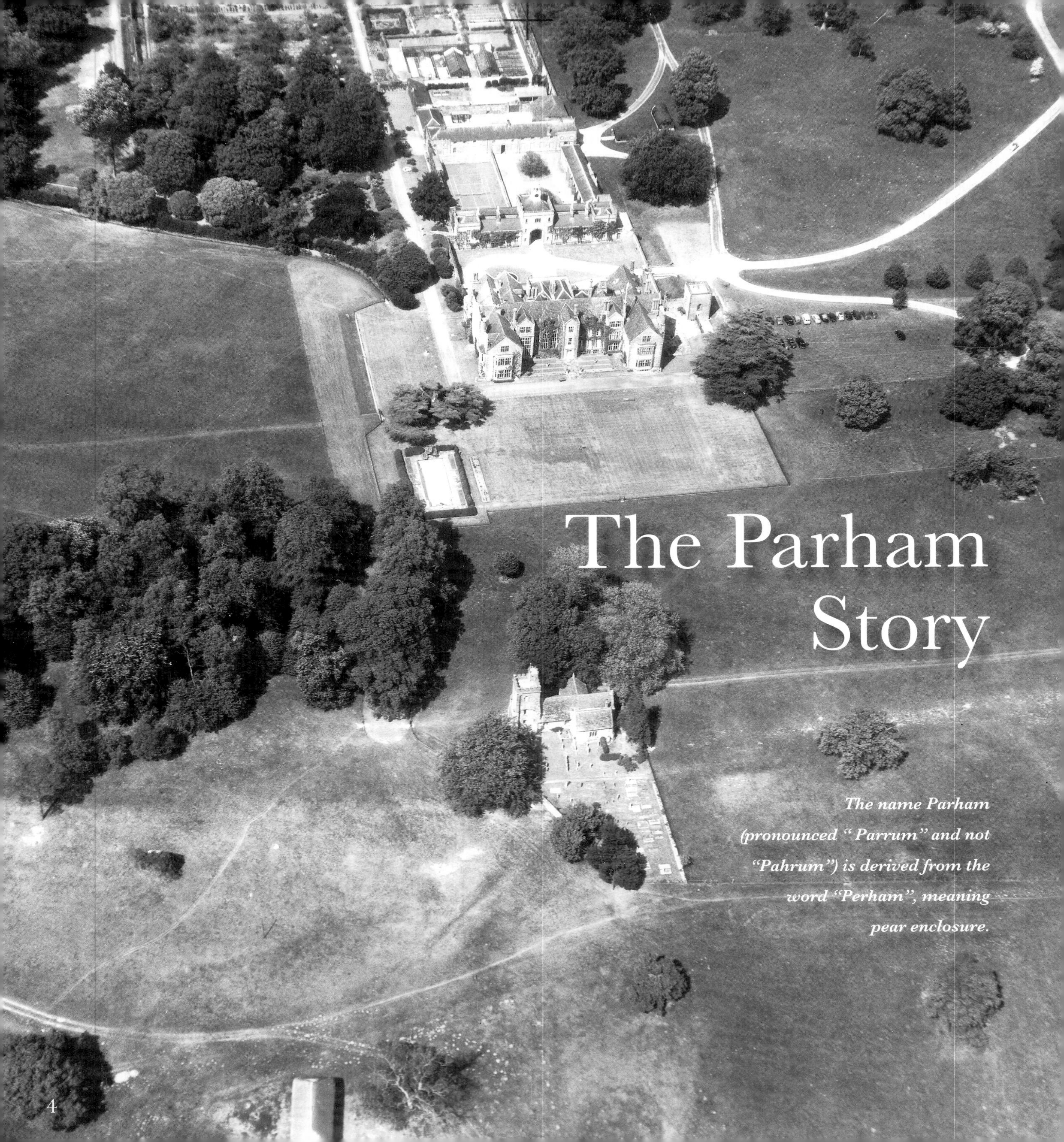

# The Parham Story

***The name Parham (pronounced "Parrum" and not "Pahrum") is derived from the word "Perham", meaning pear enclosure.***

*A Roman lead cistern was found at Wiggonholt, then part of the estate, in 1943. This is now displayed in the Long Gallery.*

# I. Early History

***A scene from a 17th century example of raised embroidery illustrating rural life, on display in the White Room.***

There is little evidence of the early history of Parham from prehistoric times until the Norman Conquest. Stane Street, the principal Roman road from Chichester to London, ran a few miles to the north west.

Domesday Book describes two estates at Parham, one held by the Monastery of Westminster and the other by Robert fitz Tetbald. By the 14th century, the fitz Tetbald estate had passed to the Tregoz family. The site of the Westminster and the Tregoz manorial buildings are unknown, but it is thought that they may only have been a few hundred metres apart.

In 1365–7 the Abbey buildings were said to comprise a thatched hall with a chamber and kitchen and a grange – probably located close to the site of the present house. There are also records of a deserted settlement immediately to the south east of the church; ***see 1950s aerial picture opposite***, but by 1778–79 these had been removed by Sir Cecil Bisshopp, the 7th Baronet, and the inhabitants relocated to nearby Rackham.

The site of the medieval village of Parham remains a mystery, but when the ha-ha was dug around the lawn to the south of the House in the late 1960s, a quantity of 13th and 14th century pottery was excavated. More recent geophysical surveys have so far produced little evidence of a village close to the church. It is therefore possible that the village of Parham was a scattered settlement which was not necessarily concentrated around the church. Research is continuing.

# II. The Palmers

In 1540, at the Dissolution of the Monastery of Westminster, Henry VIII granted the manor of Parham to Robert Palmer, a citizen and mercer of London.

Robert, who died in 1544, and his son, Sir Thomas Palmer (c.1520–1582) probably spent little time at Parham. Sir Thomas's son, William (c.1554–1586) married Elizabeth Verney of Fairfield in Somerset, a god-daughter of Elizabeth I, and they must have considered the existing house inadequate for their needs because on 28 January 1577, their 2½-year-old son Thomas laid the foundation stone of the new house, a custom that was considered to bring luck.

This little boy became Sir Thomas Palmer (1574–c.1605). He served as an adventurer with Sir Francis Drake and was knighted after the taking of Cadiz in 1596. He does not, however, appear to have had much affection for Parham, because in 1598 he leased it to Thomas Bisshopp of Henfield and eventually sold it to him in 1601 for £4,500.

*Henry VIII (detail of portrait in the Upper Lobby), and (above) his Grant of the Manor of Parham to Robert Palmer in 1540.*

*Robert Palmer asked to be buried in Parham Church and 'that a chapel should be built adjoining (the) choir there or chancel and over me a tomb be made as mine executors shall meet and honest for a remembrance of me to be had'. The chapel is now a vestry, but no trace of his monument survives.*

[illegible] gracia Anglie et Francie Rex Fidei defensor [illegible]

[illegible]omnibȝ ad quos presentes lre pvenerint : salutem : Sciatis qd nos pro summa mille ducentar quinquaginta quinqȝ librar sex solidor et quinqȝ denarior legalis monete nre
[illegible]ne nre ad usum nrm p dictm nobis Robertum Palmer Civem et Merceriu London solut de gra nra spali ac ex certa sciencia et mero motu nris dedimus et concessimus ac p presentes damus et
[illegible]tion et Wike cum eor iuribȝ membris et ptinen univsis in Com nro Sussex nup Monasterio de [illegible]isburye in Comitatu nro Glouc modo dissolut dudum spectan et ptinen ac parcell ~
[illegible]rras tenementa molendina tofta cotagia prata mariscos pasturas pasturas coias aquas piscarias [illegible] bruer boscos subboscos redditus reversiones servicia annuitates feodi firmas ~
[illegible]essionibȝ reservat [illegible] releiia Curias letas visus ffranc pleg ac omnia que ad visum franc pleg pertinent catalla [illegible] [illegible] [illegible] [illegible] ac alia iura iurisdictiones
[illegible]unqȝ cum ptinentys in Kingeston Wike et Lymyster in dicto Comitatu nro Sussex ac alibi ubicunqȝ in eodem Comitatu dictis maneriys seu eor alteri quoquo modo spectan et pertinen aut
[illegible]dita cognita capta seu reputata existen Ac unu annuu redditum tresdecim solidor et quatuor denarior exeun de omnibȝ illis terris pratis pasturis et mariscis in dicta parochia de Lymyster
[illegible]cursu maris per Edmundum Dudley Armigerum Necnon totam Rectoriam et ecclesiam ~ nram de Kyngeston cum suis iuribus et pertinentys univsis in dicto Comitatu nro Sussex dicto nup
[illegible] existen Ac advocacionem donacionem liberam disposicoem et ius patronatus vicarie ecclesie parochialis de Kyngeston in dicto Comitatu nro Sussex Necnon advocacoem donacoem et liberam
[illegible]omos [illegible] [illegible] terras glebas decimas porciones pensiones annuitates oblaciones proficua et emolumenta quecunqȝ cum ptinentys in Kingeston et alibi ubicunqȝ in dicto Comitatu nro
[illegible]eri quoquo modo spectan vel pertinen Necnon omnes et omnimodas decimas de in et super omnibȝ illis predictis terris pratis et mariscis in dicta parochia de Lymyster que ab incursu maris per
[illegible] Ac omnia alia messuagia terras tenementa prata pasturas pasturas mariscos boscos subboscos redditus reversiones servicia decimas et hereditamenta nostra quecunqȝ cum ptin in Kyngeston
[illegible]ssessionum eiusdem nuper Monasterii existen adeo plene et integre ac in tam amplis modo et forma prout ultimus Abbas dicti nuper Monasterii aut aliquis predecessor suor Abbatum eiusdem
[illegible] antequam nuper Monasterium illud ad manus nostras devenit prestit[illegible] Maneria Rectoriam advocacoem terras tenementa decimas ac cetera omnia et singula premissa superius expressa et specificat
[illegible]s fuit seu habere tenere vel gaudere debuerunt aut debuit et adeo plene et integre ac in tam amplis modo et forma prout ea omnia et singula ad manus nras racione vel pretextu ~
[illegible] per dictum nuper Abbatem et nuper Conventum dicti nuper Monasterii sub sigillo suo conventuali nobis confect aut aliter quocunqȝ modo devenerunt seu devenire debuerunt ac in manibus
[illegible]sentes concedimus [illegible] cum suis iuribus [illegible]

*Robert's son, Sir Thomas Palmer, whose grandson laid Parham's foundation stone. Sir Thomas died four years later, his son, William (right), four years after that. Robert's grandson, also a Thomas, sold the house in 1601 and he too died, coincidentally, four years later.*

*Sir Thomas's only son William married Elizabeth Verney of Fairfield House in Somerset. The two paintings above do not hang at Parham, but are reproduced by kind permission of Lady Acland Hood Gass, Fairfield House.*

# III. The Building of the House

Parham took approximately six years to build after the foundation stone was laid in 1577 by Sir Thomas Palmer's grandson.

The site of the original (smaller) house occupied by the Palmers is still unknown, and, contrary to previous thoughts, was not incorporated into the 'new' house.

Parham is a fine example of an Elizabethan H-plan, centred around the traditional Great Hall with its tall mullioned windows. The house is constructed of local sandstone known as Amberley Blue. Most of the quoins and dressings on the north and east sides are made from Pulborough sandstone, whilst those on the south and west sides are of Caen, Bath or Portland stone. The internal stonework is mainly clunch (chalk). The roof is covered with another local stone, known as Horsham 'slabs'.

Evidence suggests that the house would have been lime washed, whilst the roof timbers (which have been found by dendrochronology to date mainly from the late 1570s) would have been cut, where possible, from estate hedgerows and from 'green' oak felled from trees grown in the park. Some timbers may also have been imported from the Baltic.

***(Top): The west front of the house. This photograph also shows the ha-ha, built as a concealed barrier to the deer grazing in the park.***

***(Above): The tall mullioned windows of the Great Hall to the left of the porch date from the building of the house, but were lengthened at a later date.***

# IV. The Bisshopps

Thomas Bisshopp (c.1554 –1626), a lawyer and Member of Parliament, was knighted in 1603 and purchased a baronetcy in 1620. His son Sir Edward, 2nd Baronet, (1602–1649) was also a Member of Parliament and in 1627 gained notoriety for murdering a playwright named Henry Shirley, for which he was ultimately pardoned. Sir Edward was succeeded by his son, Sir Thomas (1627–1652). He died unmarried, and Parham passed to his brother Sir Cecil (c.1635–1705), the first of five consecutive baronets of that name.

***Above: The 19th century Gothic screen wall on the north front of the house.***

***Left: Sir Cecil, 5th Baronet (1673–1725), made various alterations to Parham, including replacing some of the 16th century windows with sashes, and he also remodelled the South Porch which bears his coat of arms.***

The 6th Baronet (1700–1778), and his wife had twelve children, eight of whom were girls. They were referred to by diarist Sir Horace Walpole as "*Sir Cecil's endless hoard of beauty daughters*". The 7th Baronet (1726–1779) only survived his father by 15 months, during which time he pulled down the remnants of the village and planned the present Mulberry Court quadrangle of offices and stables to the north of the house. The last of these Sir Cecils – the 8th Baronet (1753 –1828) became the 12th Lord Zouche, having claimed the title through his mother. He was instrumental in closing the public road through the park and replacing it with a road further to the north. He also, with the Duke of Norfolk, built the turnpike road between Storrington and Houghton Bridge to the south of the park. He spent considerable sums on modernising the house before dying heavily in debt. Parham passed to Harriett Anne (1787–1870), the eldest of his two surviving daughters. She married the Hon. Robert Curzon, the youngest surviving son of Assheton, 1st Viscount Curzon. Robert Curzon and Harriett Anne engaged the architect Anthony Salvin to carry out a remodelling. This included the construction, during the 1830s, of the Gothic style screen wall to the kitchen courtyard on the north front of the house. It is thought that the main entrance to the house was moved from the south front to its present position during the early 19th century.

Robert Curzon, the 14th Lord Zouche (1810–1873) married Emily Wilmot Horton and both held Parham in great affection. He had ambitious plans for the house but his death in 1873 meant that he had little time to carry them out. Parham and its then 3,733-acre estate were sold in 1922 by Mary, 17th Baroness Zouche (1875–1965) to the Hon. Clive Pearson for the price of £200,000. Clive Pearson and his wife Alicia were to have a profound impact on the fortunes of Parham, and their influence remains to this day.

*Sir Edward Bisshopp, 2nd Baronet, shown here with Parham House in 1632, which he inherited from his father, Sir Thomas Bisshopp.*

*He fought for the King during the Civil War. He and his wife were besieged in Arundel Castle before it was recaptured by the Parliamentarians in early 1644. He was imprisoned in the Tower of London and his estates seized.*

*The picture can be seen high up on the west wall in the Great Hall.*

Clive Pearson in 1922

# V. Clive & Alicia Pearson

Clive Pearson (1887–1965) was the second son of Weetman Dickinson Pearson, 1st Viscount Cowdray. He graduated from Cambridge with a degree in mechanical engineering, following his father into the family firm. S. Pearson and Co. was responsible, amongst many projects, for London's Blackwall Tunnel and the Southampton and Milford Haven docks. In 1917 Clive became a director of the firm, taking on the role of Chairman after his father's death in 1927. He was also Chairman of BOAC (British Overseas Airways Corporation) and a Director of the Southern Railway from 1936–1947.

*S. Pearson and Co. was one of England's foremost engineering firms, specialising in prestigious and important civil projects throughout the world, including building tunnels from New York to Long Island, draining the area around Mexico City, and carving out the country's Tehuantepec railway from the Atlantic to the Pacific.*

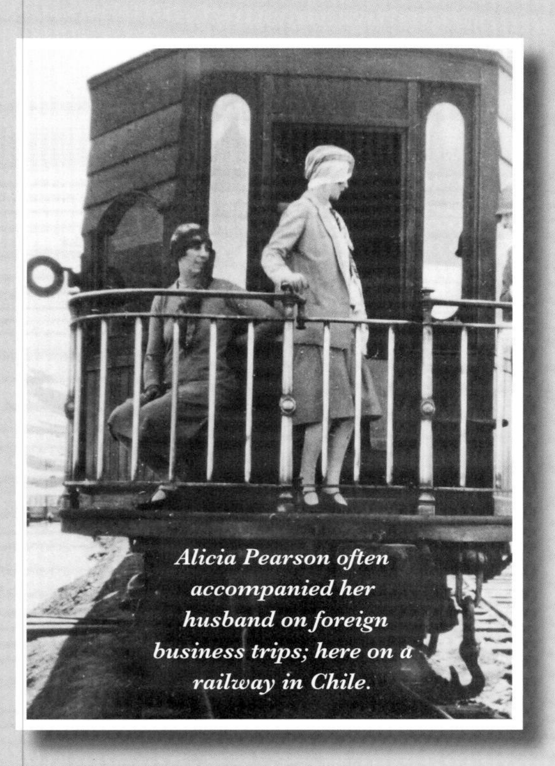
Alicia Pearson often accompanied her husband on foreign business trips; here on a railway in Chile.

In 1915 Clive married Alicia Knatchbull-Hugessen, daughter of the 1st Lord Brabourne, and in 1922, with financial help from Lord Cowdray, Clive's father, they purchased the 3,733 Parham estate for £200,000.

## Restoration & Collections

*Clive Pearson and his wife Alicia were looking for a house that needed loving care, and Parham, sad and neglected, with no drains, no electricity and a badly leaking roof, was a project they took on with great enthusiasm.*

Renovation work at Parham was carried out during the 1920s and 1930s. Clive Pearson engaged the architect Victor Heal to supervise the works, and together they oversaw the restoration of the architectural features, many of which had been covered up by previous generations.

Victorian additions were taken out and the rooms rebuilt to their original Elizabethan form. The panelling was gradually repaired and plumbing, heating and electricity were put in. Everything was done with the greatest care and sensitivity, with minute attention to detail and historical accuracy.

The Pearsons collected pictures and antique furniture with great enthusiasm, buying many things which had either once been at Parham or had an historical association with the house. They established a library and a fine portrait collection, whilst Alicia acquired a splendid collection of needlework and wool hangings.

***Below: Heal's plan for the restoration of the South Front.***

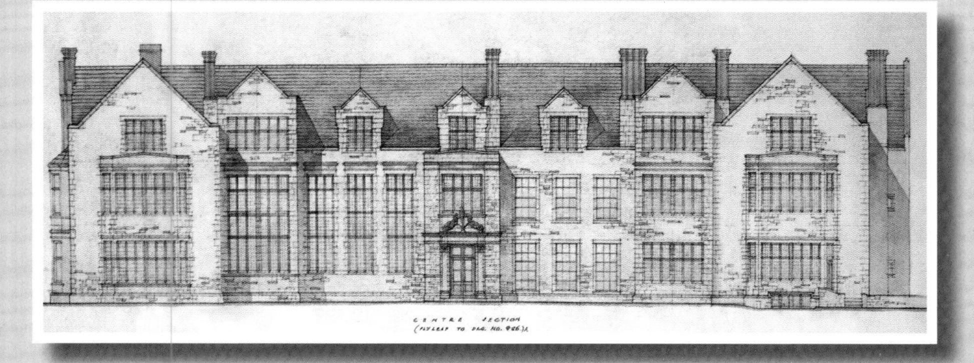

***Clive and Alicia at Parham in 1956.***

At the beginning of the Second World War in 1939 the house was re-organised, with the largest and most fragile pieces of furniture and pictures being sent into storage, and the Pearsons took in thirty evacuee children from Peckham in London.

Their eldest daughter, Veronica, took on the role of Deputy Voluntary Food Organiser for the South-Eastern Divison of the Ministry of Food, and also ran the Estate Office when her father was away on war business. The Battle of Britain took place in the skies over Parham, with dogfights overhead and sometimes aircraft crashing nearby.

***The evacuee children with their 'Hitler' snowman. Each child at Parham sent home a Christmas card of themselves. The cards are on display in the house.***

In June 1942 the War Department requisitioned the house and estate, and the evacuee children were relocated locally to make way for the 1st, 2nd and 3rd Canadian Infantry Divisions (above), in whose hands were the defences of the Sussex coast. Parham was very fortunate in its soldiers; they were engineers and could mend much of what got broken. Unlike many other houses requisitioned in the War, it survived relatively unscathed.

***Alicia Pearson (far right), with her three daughters; (left to right) Lavinia, Dione and Veronica.***

***Local instructions in the event of invasion.***

RACKHAM RECTORY,

~~May 194[illegible]~~.

I N·V A S I O N

1. If Germans actually reach this area, we are to "stay put", and not to go into the roads which will be used by the Military alone.

2. If you have urgent reason for going out for anything, only paths and fields may be used.

3. It is most important that each household should make sure of having in hand some seven days' supply of food. Always keep a stock of Flour especially (and Baking Powder), for Bread will be difficult to obtain. DO THIS NOW

4. When the Home Guard are ordered to their Stations which means actual invasion, you should go to your Food Centre (Parham House) and take with you,
   (a) The outer cover at least of your Ration Book.
   (b) Bags and baskets for carrying the tins, etc.
   (c) Money.

   The food allotted for each person costs 6/- It consists of -
   3¼ lbs. biscuits )
   1 tin corned beef )
   1 tin soup )
   1 tin condensed milk ) = 6s. 0d.
   1 lb. sugar )
   4 ozs. margarine )
   2 ozs. tea )

5. Although this supply is to be fetched by you as soon as invasion really occurs, it is not to be used until your other food has been finished. You may not need it at all in which case you should keep it most carefully and return it to the Food Officer.

6. There ought to be plenty of Milk, but you may have to fetch it yourself.

7. Apply to the Rectory at Rackham if you are uncertain what to do.

H. W. Weatherhead, Voluntary Food Officer.

Veronica Rueff, Deputy Voluntary Food Officer.

PARHAM PARK, SUSSEX

## The GREAT HALL and PRINCIPAL ROOMS

will be open

from **2 p.m.** to **6 p.m.** each **Wednesday** and **Saturday**

from **17th July** to **23rd October 1948**

also on **August Bank Holiday**

*Qualified guides in attendance.* *The last party will start at 5-15 p.m.*

Admission charge **2/6** — Children **1/6**

*Payable at the entrance*

Parking near the House, which is approached by the drive from Storrington.

---

Henry VIII, in 1540, granted Parham to Robert Palmer, whose son, Sir Thomas Palmer, built the Elizabethan house in 1577. In 1601, Sir Thomas Bysshopp purchased Parham from the Palmers, and this family lived there for three hundred years.

Parham contains much interesting furniture and needlework and an extensive collection of portraits from Elizabethan to Georgian times.

---

*Dogs not admitted*

*Left: The visitors' car park in 1956, and (above), a tour of the Great Hall in the early 1950s.*

# VII. 1948 - Parham Opens

The house was handed back to the Pearsons in 1946, and on the advice of Rupert Gunnis (an enthusiastic friend) they decided to open the house to the public – not for financial reasons, but because they wanted to share Parham with others.

Parham opened its doors on Saturday 17th July 1948, welcoming 61 visitors in its first day. Alicia, Veronica, Clive's secretary Rosemary Courcier and the Rector's wife acted as official guides, and Veronica and Alicia continued to show visitors around the house for the rest of their lives.

*Left: Veronica guiding with her characteristic verve, and (below), Alicia Pearson in the Great Hall.*

Robert PALMER was granted Parham in 1540

Sir Thomas PALMER began building Parham in 1577

William = Elizabeth Verney, god-daughter of Queen Elizabeth I

Sir Thomas laid the foundation stone of Parham in 1577 & sold the property to Sir Thomas Bisshopp in 1601

*The Arms of Weetman Dickinson Pearson, afterwards 1st Viscount Cowdray*

Sir Thomas BISSHOPP, 1st Bart. Died 1626

Sir Edward, 2nd Bart. Died 1649

Sir Thomas, 3rd Bart. Died 1652 — Sir Cecil, 4th Bart. Died 1705

# The Families of Parham

Sir Cecil, 5th Bart. Died 1725

Sir Cecil, 6th Bart. Died 1778

Sir Cecil, 7th Bart. Died 1779 = Susan Hedges. Died 1791. Descendant of Edward La Zouche, 11th Lord ZOUCHE.

Sir Cecil, 8th Bart. becoming 12th Lord Zouche of Haryngworth. Died 1828

Harriett Anne, 13th Baroness Zouche. Died 1870 = Hon. Robert CURZON, youngest son of Assheton, 1st Viscount Curzon. Died 1863

Robert, 14th Lord Zouche. Died 1873 = Emily Julia Wilmot Horton. Died 1866 — Edward. Died 1885

George. Died 1912

Robert, 15th Lord Zouche. Died 1914 — Darea, 16th Baroness Zouche. Died 1917

Mary Cecil, 17th Baroness Zouche = Sir Frederick FRANKLAND, 10th Bart. of Thirkleby. Died 1937
Sold Parham to the Hon. Clive Pearson in 1922.

Weetman Pearson, 1st Viscount Cowdray. Died 1927

Harold, 2nd Viscount. Died 1933 — Hon. Clive PEARSON. Died 1965 = Hon. Alicia Knatchbull-Hugessen, daughter of 1st Lord Brabourne. Died 1974

John, 3rd Viscount Died 1995

Michael, 4th and present Viscount

Veronica Died 1993 = (1) Marcus Rueff Died 1941 (2) Patrick TRITTON Died 1984

Lavinia Died 1991 = Major Michael Smiley Died 1991

Miranda = Benjamin Guinness, 3rd Earl of Iveagh. Died 1992 — 2 sons

Dione = Patrick, Lord Gibson Died 2004

4 sons

Lady Emma Guinness = James BARNARD — 1 daughter — 2 sons

Benjamin. Born 1996 — Arthur. Born 1998

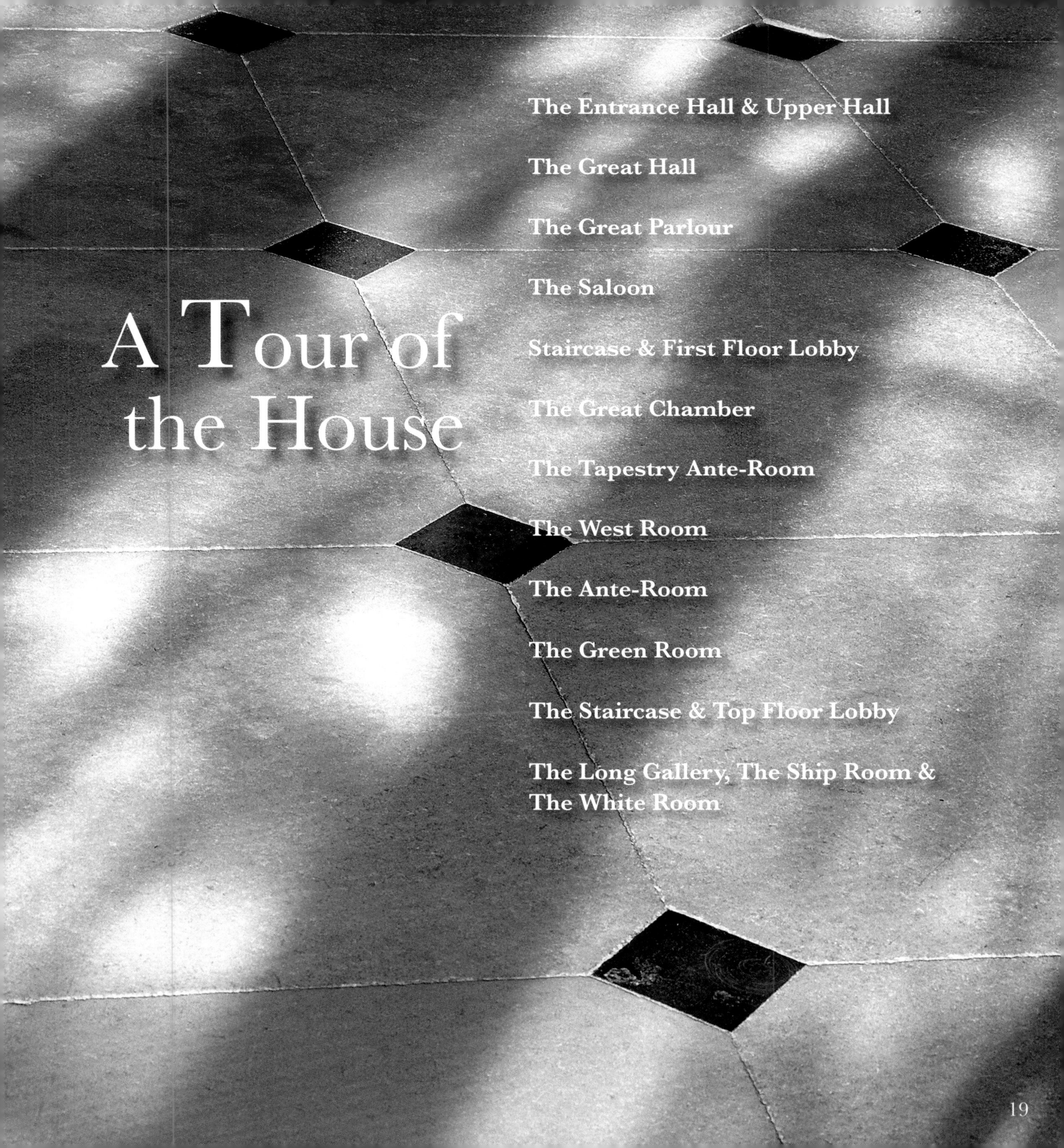

# A Tour of the House

The Entrance Hall & Upper Hall

The Great Hall

The Great Parlour

The Saloon

Staircase & First Floor Lobby

The Great Chamber

The Tapestry Ante-Room

The West Room

The Ante-Room

The Green Room

The Staircase & Top Floor Lobby

The Long Gallery, The Ship Room &
The White Room

# The Entrance Hall

*Bustard-hunting by Francis Barlow (c.1626–1702). The Great Bustard, Europe's largest game bird, was hunted to extinction in this country. Happily, it has successfully been re-introduced. Also depicted in the painting are a lapwing, a swallow, a black-headed gull, three wheatears and two herons.*

*Foxhounds with a Magpie, by John Wootton (c.1683–1764). Wootton was a renowned and successful artist specialising in rural and sporting subjects.*

*Ludovic Stuart, 2nd Duke of Lennox and 1st Duke of Richmond (1574–1624), and his third wife Frances. Stuart was cousin to James I and heir to the Scottish throne until James's children were born.*

*The painted coat of arms is that of Robert Curzon, 14th Lord Zouche, and his wife Emily Wilmot Horton (see Family Tree), whom he married in 1850; he inherited both Parham and his title from his mother. Some of Emily's drawings of Parham can be seen in the Annexe, the room to the left as you enter the front door.*

On either side of the coat of arms hangs a trophy of 19th century fallow deer antlers from the park, showing their increasing size as the buck grows year by year. The 18th century eight-day tavern clock is by John Perins, London.

# ... and The Upper Hall

At the top of the stairs, set into the wall, is a small ***marble relief of a Marine Venus by John Deare (1759–1798)***. It was brought back to Parham from Rome in 1787 by Sir Cecil Bisshopp, 8th Baronet, 12th Lord Zouche. Her toe was broken during the Canadian occupation of the house in the Second World War – one of Parham's only casualties. Below the relief is ***a painted wooden post box from the 18th century***.

Just beyond the door into the Great Hall is an 18th century oak table with a top of rare Sussex Marble – sometimes called winkle stone – in which can be seen many antediluvian crustaceans (fossils). Above it, the large painting of birds is of the 17th century Dutch School. The four leather powder buckets under the table bear the coat of arms of George III, and are dated 1795.

*"The Post Arrives at half past EIGHT And leaves at Four o'Clock"*

*Elizabeth I's 'favourite', Robert Dudley,*
*Earl of Leicester, is shown holding a petronel –*
*an early firearm – in this portrait c.1586.*
*He was commander of the English army*
*in the Netherlands at this time. He died in 1588.*

*The long case clock by J. Norris of Abingdon has stood here for over*
*two hundred years and dates from the reign of William and Mary.*

# The Great Hall

*As part of the Curzons' work on Parham during the 1830s, the floor of the Great Hall was laid and the ceiling replastered to its original pattern.*

This beautiful, light room facing south to the Downs is the heart of the house. The Elizabethan household ate their meals here on long tables with benches, some of which are still under the windows. More important members would have sat at a table on a dais across the west end.

***The Pearsons also discovered the original fireplace in 1947; it had been hidden behind three others put in in later years. On either side of this stand a pair of 18th century leather boots, which were worn by postilions – the men who rode the near horse of a pair of either two or four horses attached to a carriage or post-chaise. One boot would have been worn on the leg which went between the two horses to prevent injuries.***

The Tudor carved oak screen was put in when the house was built, and the two windows above it were rediscovered in the 1920s, having been covered up for centuries. They belonged to what was probably the steward's room. The steward's duty was to supervise the running of the household.

At the opposite (west) end of the Great Hall can be seen ***another internal window, that of the Solar or Great Chamber (below).*** This was the family's principal reception room, and from here they could see through the side window of the bay across to what in Elizabethan times would have been the front door. Parham is unusual amongst Elizabethan houses because its Great Hall is to the left of the front door, instead of to the right.

***Notice, too, the other leather items in the room – the 17th century buckets under the long bench to the right of the fireplace were used to carry water or powder in the event of a fire and the bombard (jug) on the main table is c.1655, but similar to what the Elizabethans would have used a century before.***

*The Coat of Arms high on the west wall is that of Elizabeth I. The Latin "Semper Eadem" means "Always the Same". Legend has it that the Queen dined at Parham in 1593. However, the date 1593 was incorrectly altered from 1583 when workmen were restoring the panel during the 19th century. The date 1583 probably commemorated the year when the construction of the house was completed.*

***The great draw-leaf table, with its 'melon-bulb' legs, is Elizabethan and the chairs Jacobean and Cromwellian.***

***The carved and silvered wooden chandelier dates from c.1685.***

***The Tudor oak chest – c.1555 – is the oldest piece in the house. The craftsman has carved Romanesque arches onto its front, copied from stonemasons' work he may have seen in churches.***

*Considered to be handsome, brave, loyal and generous, Robert Devereux, Earl of Essex, won the hearts of the English people, but continually quarrelled with Elizabeth I. After an ignominious campaign in Ireland he was executed in 1601.*

*Inscribed 'SAT SUPER EST' ('enough survives'), this portrait shows Henry Howard, Earl of Surrey, in the regalia of a Knight of the Garter. He carried the fourth sword at Anne Boleyn's coronation and acted at her trial in 1536. A poet with a short temper, he was often in trouble at court. He was executed in 1547 because he incorporated the Royal Coat of Arms with his own.*

*In the corner to the right of the entrance door is a narwhal's tusk, known to be over four hundred years old. Tudor and Jacobean sailors brought these back from their travels, and sold them as unicorn horns believed to have great magical and medicinal value. This one has its own original painted case.*

# Henry Frederick, Prince of Wales

by Robert Peake

*The vast portrait of Henry Frederick, Prince of Wales, was painted by Robert Peake in c.1611. The son of James I and Anne of Denmark, the Prince was hailed in his day as the great Protestant 'Hope of England'. This is symbolised in the painting by his leading of the figure of winged Time (or "Opportunity") by the forelock. Henry died tragically young of typhoid in 1612, after which the brick wall and the figure of Time were painted out. They were only rediscovered in 1985, when the picture was X-rayed in preparation for its loan to the "Treasure Houses of Great Britain" exhibition in Washington DC that year. The overpainting was then removed and the picture restored to its former glory.*

*The embroidered scenes on the richly ornamented skirt (right), show the anchor of Hope and the sun rising on a glorious future for the Protestant prince. This is considered Peake's most ambitious piece, and some believe it to be his masterpiece.*

## Some portraits of note in The Great Hall

*(Above left) William Cecil, Lord Burghley (1520–1598).*

*(Right) James I wearing the jewel "Feather".*

*(Top right) Elizabeth Palmer.*
*(Below right) Parham tradition held for many years that this was Elizabeth I. A more likely identity is Anne of Denmark, Queen of James VI of Scotland.*

*(Below left) Sir Thomas Bisshopp, 1st Baronet (c.1554–1626).*

*(Below right) Edward VI. Edward was Henry VIII's only son by his third wife, Jane Seymour.*

# The Great Parlour

This panelled room was the private sitting room. The ceiling was later removed, making it as high as the Great Hall, and so destroying the Great Chamber, or Solar, directly above. In the 19th century it was used as a billiard room.

Clive Pearson replaced the ceiling to 17 inches above its original height in 1924, and in 1935 commissioned Esmond Burton to fashion the plasterwork. Crests, charges and coats of arms from the families connected to Parham sit along the frieze and corners, and in the ceiling of the bays there are animals and birds of the period. The centre panels depict animals such as the now extinct dodo, the sea-cow (the manatee) and the South American llama, all first reported by 17th century travellers. Burton carried out all the work in the old manner, modelling the plaster with his hands using no moulds whatsoever.

***Opposite left: the entrance to the Great Parlour leading from the Great Hall. The 17th century portrait (left of the fireplace) is probably Christine of Savoy, Princess of Piedmont (1606–1663), daughter of Henry IV of France.***

***Charles I's great warship, the "Sovereign of the Seas" by L. A. Castro, hangs over the fireplace. Built at the enormous cost of £40,853 by shipwright Peter Pett, to the design of his father Phineas, and elaborately carved and decorated by the Christmas brothers, it was launched in 1637, but destroyed by the fire from a candle in the cook's cabin in 1696.***

***Charles I (1600–1649) on horseback After Sir Anthony Van Dyck 1599–1641).***

*All the portraits in this room are 17th century.*

*(Left): Traditionally called Elizabeth of Bohemia, "The Winter Queen" (1596–1662) was the sister of Charles I, and married Frederick, the Elector Palatine. They were the grandparents of George I.*

*(Top right, opposite): "An Infanta of Spain" by Juan Pantoja de la Cruz (c.1553–1608).*

*(Below, opposite): Attributed to William Larkin (c.1585–1619), depicts "A Lady" of the period.*

*(Far right, opposite): Susan Villiers, Countess of Denbigh, the sister of James I's favourite, George, Duke of Buckingham, by William Larkin. It is situated between the windows.*

*In the two full-length portraits one can see the subjects wearing rings on their left hands, attached to black silk threads or perhaps kid leather thongs. It is thought that these could be worn either to draw attention to the ring, or to hold the ring on the finger.*

Villers

***Charles I when Prince of Wales by Daniel Mytens. The Prince is seen in 1623 soon after his return from his clandestine visit to Spain with the Duke of Buckingham, having failed to secure the hand of the Spanish Infanta, Maria Anna. Although clean shaven in this portrait, he introduced the Spanish fashion for gentlemen to wear beards.***

***Henrietta Maria, Charles I's Queen, by Adriaen Hanneman. Born in the Louvre, youngest daughter of Henry IV of France, she married Charles at just 15. After initial unhappiness, they went on to have a long and happy marriage. She died in 1669.***

The subjects of all the other portraits in the room are connected to Charles either by blood or by marriage. ***The double equestrian portrait (opposite right) by Claude Deruet is The Triumph of Louis XIII of France with his wife, Anne of Austria, after the siege and capture of Nancy in 1633.*** The engraving next to the portrait of an unknown Spanish princess in the west bay window is of Charles I and the Spanish Infanta, Maria Anna, anticipating 'the Marriage-That-Never-Took-Place'. This refers to Charles's attempt in 1623 to arrange a marriage between himself and Maria Anna.

The needlework, tapestry and carpets are 17th century. The carpets are Kouba and Shirvan, the tapestry on the settee and armchairs is Flemish. The lacquered longcase clock at the other end of the room is by Bowly, London, c.1730 and is decorated with scenes from the novel Don Quixote.

***Pot pourri – lavender, pomanders and rose leaves – sits in an 18th century Chinese cistern in the window.***

***The armchair is one of a pair dating from the late 17th century. The back and seats are covered in gros and petit point needlework.***

# The Saloon

This room is said to have once been used as a wood store – notice the doors leading in all directions. In about 1790 it was remodelled as an elegant drawing room by Cecil Bisshopp, 8th Baronet, 12th Lord Zouche.

*The 8th Baronet's son, Cecil, never inherited Parham; he went abroad with his regiment in 1812, died during the American War of 1812–1814 and is buried under an oak tree at Stamford near Niagara Falls. A pastel portrait of him when a boy, with his sister Katherine Annabella and their dog, hangs to the right of the main bookshelves.*

The needlework on the early 18th century winged armchair was copied exactly onto a modern reproduction by Alicia Pearson and her mother Ethel, Lady Brabourne, in 1924. The modern colours have faded, whilst the vegetable dyes used in the original have remained much more vivid. Two embroidered cushions sit on the Queen Anne walnut window seat. One is 17th century, worked in Hungarian Point, the other 18th century with a design of red cypress trees.

*The Worcester dinner service (Barr, Flight and Barr marks) was given as a wedding present by the 8th Baronet to his eldest son Cecil (the little boy with the dog, above right), when he married Lady Charlotte Townshend in 1805.*

*A view of the Thames by William James.*

*'Winter', and 'Summer', two of The Four Seasons.*

Two 18th century views of London and the Thames by William James hang opposite the windows. On either side of the fireplace hang an early 19th century set of engravings depicting The Four Seasons, by J.C. Stadler after Adam Buck. The five portraits by G.H. Harlow are of the actor John Fawcett with his family. Fawcett was stage manager of Covent Garden in 1829. The Canton lacquer cabinet to the right of the fireplace dates from c.1820, and the double pedal action harp was patented by Sebastian Erard in April 1811. The painted beechwood chairs are Sheraton.

***Opposite: a close up of one of Fawcett's boys, showing Harlow's fluid oil technique; and (below), a portrait of their mother.***

*Visiting ornithologists to the house may find the small collection of waterfowl pictures of interest; two small studies of Mallard and Shoveler ducks below a unique oil of a Red-necked grebe in winter plumage.*

*Reflected in the looking glass is the portrait of Mary Bisshopp as 'Diana', with her greyhound.*

*A rare George II walnut and gilt framed mirror hangs above an 18th century console table with a simulated marble top.*

# Staircase & First Floor Lobby

The staircase rises round a massive square of soft limestone, known as clunch. As you go up, an Afshar rug hangs on the wall and ***an early 17th century painting (right) of the Countess of Thanet, Sir Edward Bisshopp's mother-in-law, shows her wearing a long blackwork dress.*** In the First Floor Lobby, ***an early 18th century walnut china cabinet contains part of a Bloor Derby dinner service of c.1820***. The 17th century armchair is covered with 20th century needlework; above it hangs a George II needlework panel of flowers worked in silk and wool. The red and gold candlestand (now a lamp) is Italian, from the 17th century.

On the other side of the clock is a portrait of Mary, daughter of Sir Cecil Bisshopp, the 5th Baronet (he died in 1725). Painted by Alexis Simon Belle, she is depicted as the Goddess Diana, attended by her greyhound and wearing a crescent moon in her hair. Round the corner in the Passage is a portrait of the 1st Viscount Curzon's third wife, Anna Margaretta Meredith; she is the child on her mother Johanna Cholmondeley's knee. ***A touching pair of Curzon family pictures hang to the left of the William and Mary longcase clock. They depict the first and second wives of Assheton, 1st Viscount Curzon; Esther with their three children and Dorothy with their seven. Three of the babies have died, and are sitting in a cloud.***

Opposite the rare 18th century East Indian printed cotton hangings is a pair of pictures by Luttichuys of Charles II, as yet uncrowned, and of his brother the Duke of York, later James II, painted in Holland in 1660, immediately before the Restoration. This floor originally formed part of the Elizabethan Solar, or Great Chamber. The little window looking down into the Great Hall would once have been part of this room. A view of the Great Hall hangs next to this window, drawn in c.1860 by Emily Curzon. The lady in the blue dress at the end of the passage is Elizabeth Finch, by Sir Peter Lely (1618–1680).

# The Great Chamber

The Great Chamber was much larger and higher in Tudor and Stuart times and was the family's main reception room. It was remodelled in 1924 to become Alicia Pearson's bedroom. Esmond Burton did the plasterwork. Upon the fireback are the arms of Sir Weetman Pearson, later 1st Viscount Cowdray, Clive Pearson's father. On either side of the fireplace hang a pair of full-length portrait panels c.1688 of James II worked in cross and tent stitch; the King is wearing the ribbon of the Garter. The walnut firescreen frames a panel of Queen Anne needlework. The baby chair dates from c.1660 and has always been at Parham.

***The frame of the Great Bed is partly Tudor, probably from the court of Henry VIII. The two sets of curtains, pelmets and valances with flame stitch embroidery date from c.1620. Its embroidered canopy, backcloth, headboard and bedspread are of French or Italian workmanship and date from c.1585. Interwoven monograms and the fleur-de-lys suggest that this might have been commissioned by Marie de Medici – the figure on the headboard is said to resemble a portrait of Marie by Rubens. The Great Bed came to Parham from Wroxton Abbey in Oxfordshire.***

***The portraits around the bed are of various members of the Dering family; a Dering descendant, Harriett Anne Southwell, married Sir Cecil Bisshopp, 8th Baronet and 12th Lord Zouche. Alicia Pearson and Lady Emma are directly descended from Harriett Anne's great-great aunt Mary, so the Derings form a link between the past and present families at Parham.***

A Koula rug lies under the winged settee which is covered with 18th century needlework. The pair of gesso stools on either side of it are George II, with mid-18th century needlework seats. The large carpet with floral medallions is a Persian Hamadan. In the south window the side-table is Jacobean. On it stands a Stuart fish skin writing case and a pair of silvered candlesticks c.1750. Beneath is a red Turkish Ghiordes carpet; two 18th century Ghiordes rugs lie on either side of the bed. On the right of the bed is a Charles II chest of drawers inlaid with bone and mother of pearl. The inlaid bracket clock is by Bowly, London. On the left of the bed a small 17th century Italian walnut marquetry travelling chest sits on another inlaid chest of drawers.

# The Great Chamber

*An Elizabethan table in the centre between two stools of the same period, supports a case with a particularly fine needlework cushion of the finding of Moses, from the Stuart period (signed M.L. 1644)*

*The lacquered cabinet by the windows dates from c.1700, with a silvered stand and cresting. An 18th century Chinese punchbowl showing the arms of Beckford stands on top of it. A fine set of Charles II walnut dining chairs stand around the room.*

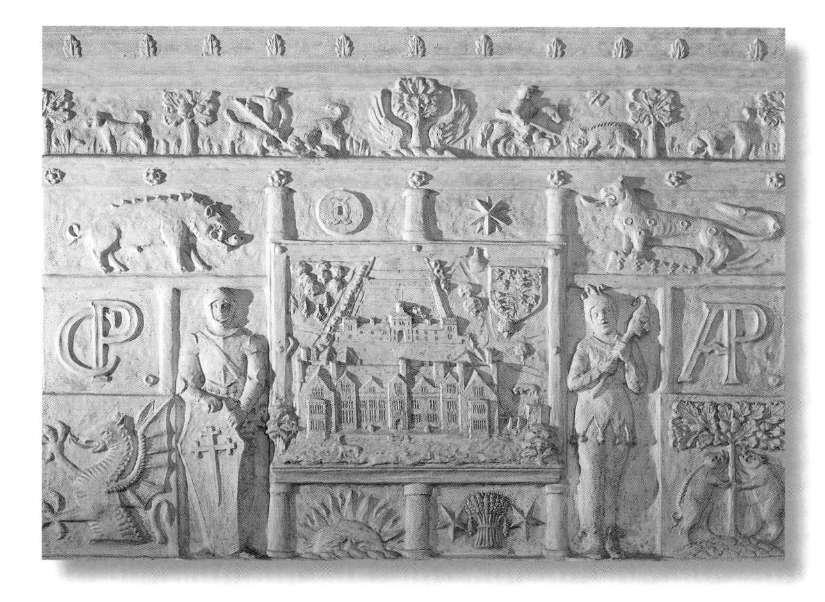

*The plasterwork overmantel shows the initials of Clive and Alicia Pearson 'CP' and 'AP'. Amongst the emblems which surround the view of the house, which has Elizabeth I's arms beside it, are crests and various charges from their coat of arms.*

*In The Great Chamber … and in the Great Chamber Corridor.*

*General George Monck, Duke of Albemarle KG (1608–1670) by Wright. After a successful career as a professional soldier, he fought for Charles I in the Civil War. He was captured and incarcerated in the Tower of London, before being released by Cromwell to serve the Parliamentary forces. He raised the Coldstream Guards and was instrumental in the Restoration of Charles II.*

*Charles II and his brother James, Duke of York (right), by Dutch artist Simon Luttichuys (1610–1661).*

*Before the West Room, there is the Tapestry Ante-Room. Formerly a bathroom, it now holds a 16th century Brussels tapestry, and two further Flemish 17th century tapestries to the right.*

## Sir Cecil Bisshopp, 4th Baronet (c.1635–1705) and his son Sir Cecil Bisshopp, 5th Baronet (1673–1725)

*In 1698, Sir Cecil, 5th Baronet (right), married heiress Elizabeth Dunch, daughter of Henry Dunch of Newington, Oxfordshire, thus adding the estate of Newington and other Oxfordshire properties to the Bisshopp family. The portraits are by Sir Godfrey Kneller (left) and Jonathan Richardson (right).*

# The West Room

# The West Room

The portraits of Sir Edward Dering and his wife Mary hang in the centre of the wall opposite the window. They are the common ancestors of the later Curzons and of the Pearsons. The other portraits are of ancestors closely connected to the house.

On the walls hang a set of late 16th century Italian wool hangings, possibly the earliest attempts at the Flame Stitch design (1560–85). On the floor is a very rare 17th century striped Armenian Kouba carpet. The needlework picture of Adam and Eve is Elizabethan; the beadwork picture, by the door, is Stuart.

The furniture in this room is English. The early 18th century triangular oak table is for the card game "ombre"; the seaweed-marquetry stick barometer is about the same date. The chairs date from c.1740 (the wide seats of some of them were made to accommodate the male fashions of the day). The longcase clock is by E. Stanton, London (Master of the Clockmakers Company 1696–1701). The perambulating survey wheel or "waywiser" was made in c.1790 by G.Adams, London.

The blue Chinese baluster vase and the figures of Immortals are Ming. The triangular flint-glass paperweights, prismatically cut and painted with flowers, are Victorian; ones of this kind were invented by John Rose in 1840. They were made with a special white sand, imported from Sydney, Australia, in the form of ballast carried by the wool-laden sailing ships of the day. The clear and brilliant glass produced is free of the impurities which are normally seen in tinted flint-glass of this period. They were in great demand as beneath candlelight and gas-light rainbow colours were reflected very vividly.

***Henry Bisshopp lived at Parsonage House, a family property in Henfield. In 1643, Parliamentary troops searched the house to arrest him, as he was a known Royalist sympathiser. He hid in a hole in the floor of a bedroom, with his dog, Charles. Remarkably, the dog remained still and quiet and so they avoided detection. This painting commemorates this event. After escaping to Virginia, America, for two years, he returned at the Restoration, whereupon Charles II granted him the office of Postmaster General for seven years. Bisshopp found the work too taxing and asked to be relieved of the position after only three. However, his lasting legacy was his introduction of the 'Bisshopp mark', to be stamped on letters – the forerunner of our modern stamp.***

***The walnut tallboy was made c.1750.***

The double portrait over the chimney piece is of Sir Ralph Assheton of Whalley (died 1679) and Elizabeth Harrington, his 2nd wife, painted by Sir Peter Lely. He was connected to both the Derings and the Bisshopps through his first wife. Elizabeth ran away from him and after her return he had this picture painted to show him holding a lock of her hair, with his foot on her dress – perhaps a reminder to her not to try to escape again.

Sr Raphe Afsheton
of Whalley Bart Brother
of Lady Afsheton of Middleton
Lady Curzon's Grandmother.
And— Harrington,
Daughter of Sr Sapcote Harrington,
his second Lady.–
By Sr P. Lelev.

The Ante-Room

Almost everything is this room is 17th century, including the large gros-point carpet which is thought to be English. This is one of the earliest surviving examples of needlework carpets, and the only example of an embroidered carpet in the house. The cross stitch is worked in wool on canvas. On the walls behind hang some beautiful Hungarian Point needlework curtains in silk and wool. The two late 17th century walnut armchairs are covered with contemporary needlework.

***The portrait of Charles II (right) in Garter robes*** is by Simon Verelst, a famous Dutch flower painter. Sir Peter Lely's ***portrait of Charles's mistress Barbara Villiers, Lady Castlemaine, Duchess of Cleveland, hangs to his left (main picture, opposite left). A portrait of another of his mistresses, Louise de Kéroualle, Duchess of Portsmouth (over the page).***

## *Charles II – his Mistresses and his Queen*

***A picture of Charles's Queen, Catherine of Braganza, (right), by Sir Peter Lely,*** hangs over the doorway. By the window hangs a portrait of Anne Hyde, the first wife of the King's brother, James II.

***On the low oak table (opposite page), sits a copy of Littleton's Dictionary, dedicated to the King.*** A contemporary impression in lead of the King's Great Seal hangs on the right of the fireplace. In the overmantel niche sits an early 19th century Staffordshire pottery Enoch Wood figure of Fortitude.

## Louise De Kéroualle
### Duchess of Portsmouth
(1644–1721)

Louise arrived in England from France in 1670 as maid of honour to Charles II's sister, Henrietta, and swiftly became the King's mistress.

In 1672 she gave birth to a son, the last of Charles II's natural children, who was created the Duke of Richmond. He later acquired Goodwood, where his descendants still reside.

*Over the sideboard is a portrait by Northcote of Omiah, the Otaheitan chief, who came to England with Captain Cook. He was the first South Sea islander to visit Europe. Banks can also be seen in the colour engraving nearby of The Woburn Sheepshearing, 1804 – he is on the extreme right, seated on a chair.*

*Frances Bisshopp, Lady Warren by Romney*

*Kangaroo by Stubbs*

*Omiah by James Northcote RA*

# The Green Room

*David Garrick by Vandergucht*

*Emma Hamilton by Romney*

*Dingo by Stubbs*

# The Green Room

The contents of this room centre round Sir Joseph Banks, President of the Royal Society (1744–1820), the great botanist and naturalist who was largely responsible for founding Kew Gardens.

Banks is pictured as a young man, wearing a New Zealand mantle and surrounded by objects from New Zealand and Polynesia, in the print to the left of the curtained doorway. Below this hangs a mezzotint of a portrait of Banks by Sir Joshua Reynolds. This was painted just after his return from Captain Cook's first voyage round the world in "Endeavour" in 1768–71. From this adventure Banks brought back the skin of a kangaroo, and asked his friend the painter George Stubbs (1724–1806) to make a picture of the animal as best he could. Stubbs cleverly inflated the skin and the result is the delightful picture in this room, the first likeness of a kangaroo to be seen in Europe. Stubbs painted the companion picture of a dingo dog at the same time.

*Above the fireplace is a beautiful seascape of Dutch Men O'War Becalmed off a Coast by Samuel Scott, signed and dated 1732 on a floating spar. A painting of a 19th century Land Yacht hangs above it. Clive Pearson used to sail a land yacht on the West Plain, which you can see from the windows.*

*On the left of the fireplace is a portrait by Thomas Gainsborough of Major Norton Knatchbull in the uniform of the 21st Royal North British Fusiliers. His niece Joan Knatchbull, painted by George Romney, hangs on the right.*

A small needlework picture shows Banks presenting Omiah to Queen Charlotte and four of the Princesses. Above this is an oval engraving of Banks's wife, Dorothea Hugessen, whose sister was an ancestor of Lady Emma Barnard through her great-grandmother Alicia Pearson. At the top hangs a Bartolozzi stipple engraving of Nathaniel Dance's drawing of Omiah.

Framed on the wall by the window is plate 133 of the 735 engravings in *Banks's Florilegium*, which records all the plants collected by Banks and Solander on their voyage with Captain Cook. Beneath this is John Preston Neale's watercolour of Banks's house, Spring Grove at Isleworth, signed and dated 1815.

Several other portraits not bearing a direct relation to Sir Joseph Banks also hang in the room; two by Romney of Lord Nelson's love Emma Hamilton and of Frances Bisshopp, Maid of Honour to Queen Charlotte; the famous 18th century actor David Garrick holding a medallion of Shakespeare and the wand of office as Steward of the Stratford Jubilee of 1769; a Reynolds portrait of John Crauford, M.P. for Old Sarum – a "rotten borough" only containing two buildings, one of which was Stonehenge.

A watercolour of the Green Room painted by Emily Curzon in c.1863 hangs just outside the door.

***On the floor are two terrestrial globes, the larger one dedicated to Banks and dated 1807. This does not show the south coast of Australia, marked as 'New Holland', as it had not yet been mapped.***

***Omiah is also pictured to the right of the curtained doorway in this sepia drawing (after the painting by William Parry) of Banks introducing him to his Swedish secretary and librarian Dr Daniel Solander, the famous botanist.***

***The caption reads; 'Omai, – Sir Joseph Banks, – Dr Solander – From the original picture, painted by Wm Parry Esq RA - , in the possession of Sir Robt Williams Vaughan Bart – Wm Parry was pupil to Sir Joshua Reynolds and died in London March 1791'.***

***Lady Curzon***
*with her two sons*
***Nathaniel***
***&***
***Assheton***
*by Andrea Soldi,*
*1738*

***Nathaniel (left) went on to be created 1st Baron Scarsdale. Assheton's younger son, Robert, by his second wife Dorothy, married Harriett Bisshopp, 13th Baroness Zouche in 1808.***

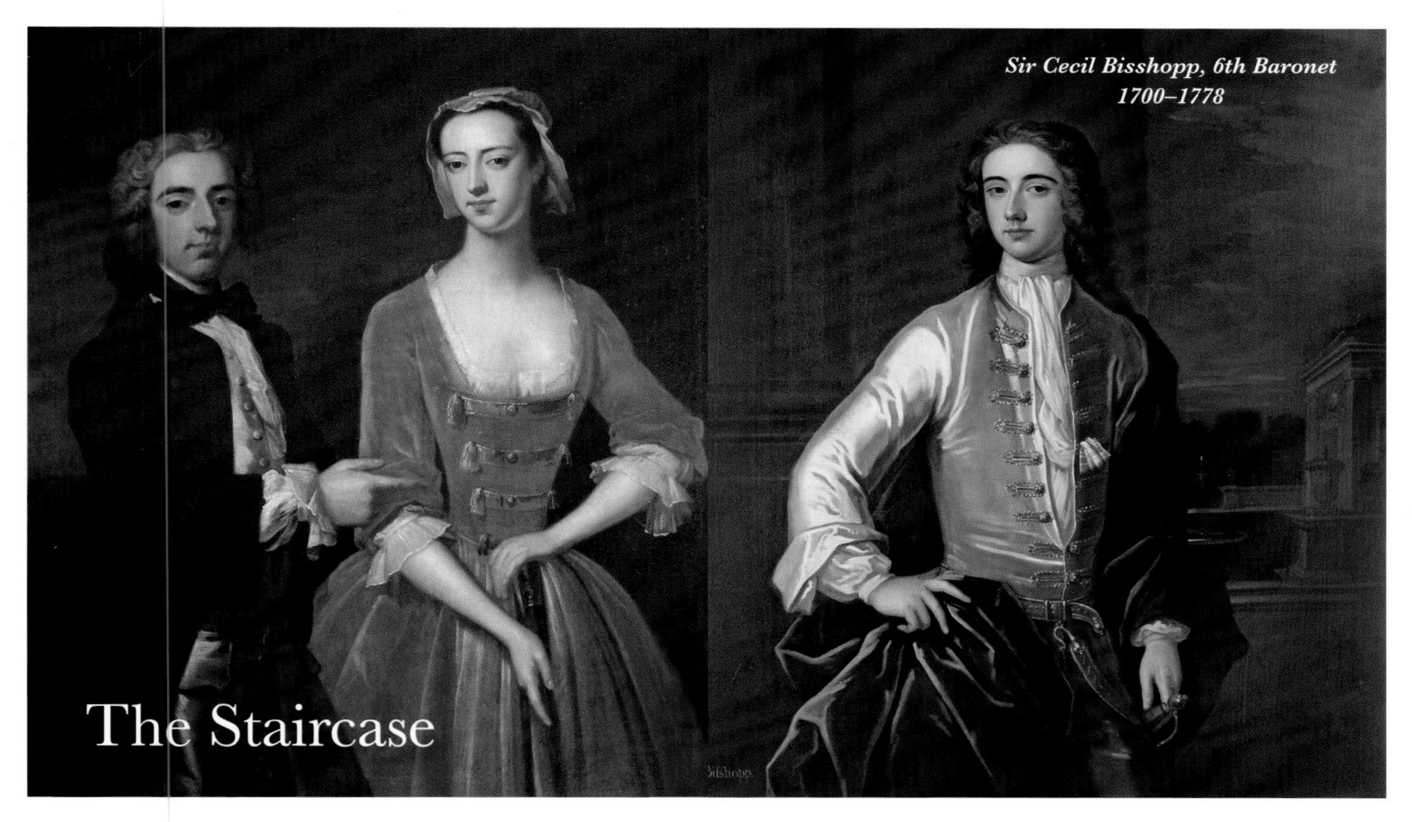

*Sir Cecil Bisshopp, 6th Baronet*
*1700–1778*

# The Staircase & Top Floor Lobby

***The double portrait towards the top is of Sir Cecil Bisshopp, 6th Baronet, and his wife Ann Boscawen, daughter of 1st Viscount Falmouth. He planted many of the trees in the North Park at Parham. Their son Cecil, 7th Baronet, of whom there is no portrait, was responsible for planning the stables, courtyards and laundry buildings with the clock tower to the north of the house. He also removed what remained of the village of Parham.***

***A 17th century reclining chair.***

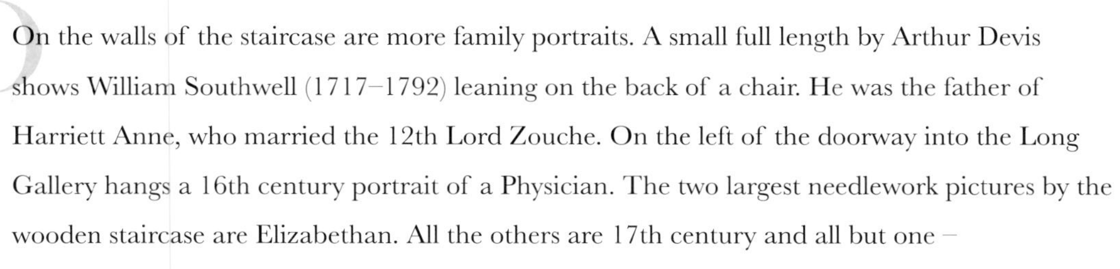

On the walls of the staircase are more family portraits. A small full length by Arthur Devis shows William Southwell (1717–1792) leaning on the back of a chair. He was the father of Harriett Anne, who married the 12th Lord Zouche. On the left of the doorway into the Long Gallery hangs a 16th century portrait of a Physician. The two largest needlework pictures by the wooden staircase are Elizabethan. All the others are 17th century and all but one – Diana and Actaeon – are of religious subjects, including a Bible cover worked with metal thread as well as silk. A splendid portrait after Holbein of Henry VIII hangs to the right of the door to the Long Gallery.

*Carved and painted arms of King William III and Queen Mary.*

This extraordinary room is 158 ft long (48 metres) and is the third longest in England.

Long Galleries were used for a range of activities including entertaining, promenading, displaying portraits and tapestries and even sleeping!

The wide oak floorboards and lightly waxed oak wainscot panelling are Jacobean. The original panelling was saved by the Pearsons after the removal of many layers of later decoration. A panel to the left of the entrance door shows this process. There was once a chapel off the north east end. This end of the gallery itself was partitioned and used as a nursery for the Pearson children.

## The Long Gallery

***To the right of the Ship Room – containing an exhibition about the Pearson family and life at Parham between 1922 and 1948 – stands a Roman marble statue of a woman from the 1st century AD. It is thought to be the Goddess Isis.***

***The spectacular ceiling was put in by the Pearsons between 1962 and 1968. There is no record of the original Elizabethan ceiling and they decided to add something from the 20th century as their contribution to the house. Oliver Messel designed it and the decoration is painted on squares of canvas glued to the plaster. The design reflected the family's connection with Sir Joseph Banks.***

*In a south alcove in the centre of the Gallery is a fine 17th century spinet by Johannes Wilbrook, London. On the wall is a charango. From the windows there are fine views of the South Downs and the Church.*

*Above, opposite: At the end of the Gallery is a fine collection of embroidered furniture. On the north wall can be seen a family tree of James I of England and VI of Scotland; those who are married are holding hands!*

*Top right: A portrait of the author Fanny Burney by her cousin, Edward Burney.*

***James II's velvet and silver gilt embroidered State saddle created for his visit to Bristol in 1686.***

# The White Room

The White Room, at the north-west end, contains the main collection of Parham's 17th century needlework and stump work pictures. The room was once the nursery of Robert and Darea Curzon, who can be seen in the two portraits by Alexander Glasgow, with their parents Robert and Emily Curzon.

A portrait by Harlow of Emily's mother, Lady Anne Horton, hangs above the cradle. She inspired Byron to write 'She walks in Beauty, like the Night…'

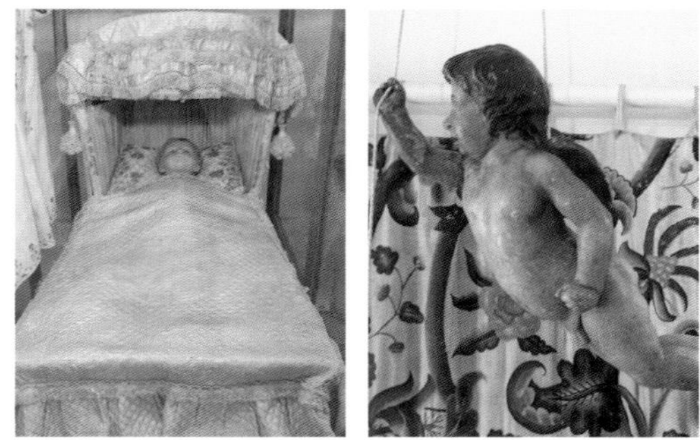

***Above left: A mid-Victorian wax doll in a cradle with contemporary and 18th century needlework.***

***Above right: The cover of the Jacobean carved front depicting Adam and Eve is counter-balanced by a cherub suspended on a rope over a pulley.***

*Detail from James II's saddle in the Long Gallery.*

Parham has one of the finest and most important collections of 17th century embroidery in the country.

# Needlework & Tapestry

The range of objects embraces an unparalleled group of Stuart embroidered pictures and panels, together with covers for furniture, room hangings, bed hangings of the most remarkable quality, horse furniture, samplers and many other items executed by both amateur and professional embroiderers.

In addition to the 17th century collection, representative examples of work for the 18th, 19th and 20th centuries are also to be found throughout the house, and the entire collection is complemented by the many portraits containing a wealth of needlework detail.

***Top: A late 18th century silkwork picture of a rabbit or hare in a thicket.***

***Above: The Judgement of Solomon.***

***Below: A section from a 'rebozo', a Mexican embroidered shawl.***

The Kitchen, or "Big Kitchen", as it is known, still retains many of its Elizabethan features, but the range made by Benham and Sons of London dates from the 1920s. There is also a fine collection of *batterie de cuisine* and copperware. The walled garden and estate farm provided meat and produce, and the park supplied game and venison. The Parham recipe book (see front endpaper) contains a number of fascinating dishes and cures for ailments.

Parham has not entertained many royal or famous visitors over the centuries. There are no existing accounts of Elizabeth 1st's reputed visit but Princess Charlotte, the daughter of the Prince Regent, visited in 1808 and the Duchess of Kent with the young Princess Victoria in 1821.

When Queen Mary came in 1928 she took a wrong turning and made her entrance in the royal car via a farmyard!

***These paintings by Peter Brears are conjectural and depict the Big Kitchen and the Great Hall as they may have appeared during the early 17th Century.***

***The Big Kitchen seen illustrated here from left: the pastry oven, the open fire for boiling the food for those in the Great Hall and the roasting hearth for the meats served to the family and guests. The man to the left of the right hand fireplace is sharpening his knife on the stonework of the arch.***

***In many respects the Great Hall today is little altered in appearance from what we see below. The marshall is seen leading the waiters with the food to the 'top' table, where the steward, clerks and other senior officers would sit. The family would have taken meals in the privacy of their own dining parlour, except on special occasions.***

# The Household & Entertaining

***Life in the 1930s at Parham: Alicia Pearson with the chauffeur, Mr Petre, and Lavinia Pearson in the Fountain Courtyard, with the butler, Mr Cridland.***

# The South Front

# The Gardens & Parkland

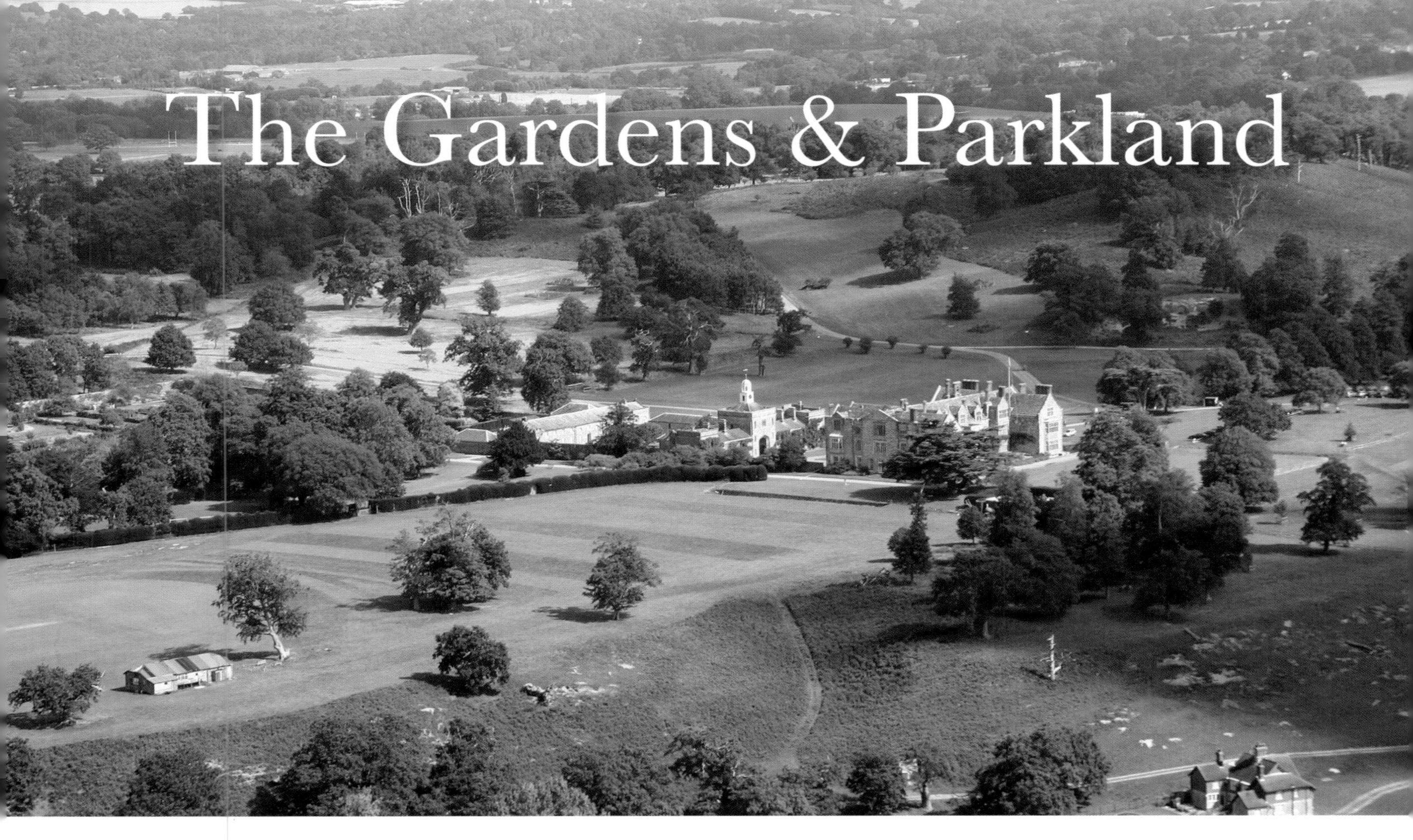

*The Parham Estate comprises a total of 354 hectares (875 acres) of working agricultural and forestry land, including an area of parkland designated as a Site of Special Scientific Interest. The SSSI is about 137 hectares (338 acres) and includes the deer park.*

*There are 1.6 hectares (4 acres) of Walled Garden and a further 2.8 hectares (7 acres) of Pleasure Grounds around the house.*

*The present parkland is a remarkable survival of a 17th century deer park, but it is also the product of the later Georgian and Regency eras. The landscape was not moulded by one of the fashionable designers of the period, although their influence did not completely bypass Parham. Tree planting schemes, including clumps of fir, still survive. It is possible that the sand pit or quarry, which can be seen to the east of the house, may have been intended as a 19th century 'picturesque' feature.*

# The Walled Garden

Few documents survive which give us any idea of the past history of the Walled Garden. There would have been a garden in the place from earliest times, but it is only since the 1920s that its history has been recorded.

Approximately four acres in size, the soil is predominantly Lower Greensand, sandy and slightly acid, easy to work, but quick to dry out. Until the late 1970s the garden was predominantly a 'working' one, providing vegetables, fruit and cut flowers for the house.

Early in the 1980s, the designer Peter Coates was brought in. Noted for his striking use of colour, his borders were a mixture of shrubs and herbaceous plants.

The late Ray Gibbs took over in 1990 as Head Gardener and, in partnership with Joe Reardon-Smith, continued to create new planting schemes . This is, of course, an ongoing process.

***The Walled Garden's walls vary in age. Some parts date from the 18th century.***

Gardens change. They alter, develop and decay. Parham's garden has been cultivated for many hundreds of years, and our only 'rule' is to work with, and not against, this ancient place – accepting and preserving its spirit. The garden's tranquillity surely reflects the hours of labour and love put into it across the centuries.

# The Entrance Borders

A long vista leads from wrought iron gates guarded by Istrian stone lions to a classical summer house at the northern end containing some sad marble putti – probably rescued from the churchyard from an unknown 17th century tomb. The two low walls, planted with clematis and roses, were built in memory of Clive Pearson.

# The Blue & Gold Borders

The Blue Borders are backed by espaliered apple trees. Halfway down are some of the many dipping ponds to be found all over the garden. Constructed in the 1920s, they were originally linked by pipes to supply the gardens with fresh running water. At the west end of the Blue Borders is the Bell Door, so-called because a bell used to be hung here to summon the family into the house. It leads out into the Pleasure Grounds. To the east, the colours of the Gold Borders echo the tiled roof of the 18th-century dovecote behind the wall.

# The Herb Garden

Enclosed by a yew hedge, its circular stone pond is surrounded by medieval and Tudor culinary, healing and strewing herbs.

## The Lavender Garden

Designed to celebrate the Millennium, this garden was created from an area that was once a giant fruit cage. A simple St George's Cross of lavender vera, its quarters are planted with varieties of hazel and cobnut. Once flowering is over in late spring, the grass is left to grow and flower, and by August, when the lavender begins, it is a soft gold.

## The Orchard

In gentle maturity, almonds, sweet chestnuts and walnut trees have been added. Some of the apple trees are festooned with mistletoe.

## The Rose Garden

This garden contains many deliciously scented Old Shrub roses underplanted with white Regal lilies, and is at its peak in June and July.

## The Vegetable Garden

Designed in the 1990s to be both pretty and practical, the Vegetable Garden houses an eclectic mix of vegetables and flowers. The produce is used by those who live and work at Parham.

***To the south of the Vegetable Garden, in a small grassed enclosure, lies a Carrara marble statue of a dying soldier. This is signed 'L. Amigoni, Bergamo 1857' and was exhibited at the Great Dublin Exhibition in the late 19th century. It was brought to Parham from Dublin by Lady Emma in 2000.***

# The Greenhouse & Wendy House

The garden buildings were designed by Victor Heal in the 1920s. The greenhouse is all that now remains of a connecting series of four, built by Mackenzie and Moncur of Edinburgh in 1923. Today, it supplies the garden with a range of seedlings in addition to growing plants and shrubs more suited to indoor conditions.

The Wendy House was built into the garden wall in 1928 for Clive Pearson's three daughters, Veronica, Lavinia and Dione. It is a perfect child-sized cottage, with an oak front door, wrought iron balcony, fireplace and a beautifully made wooden staircase inside. Lady Emma and her family have a tradition of spending at least one summer's night here, lighting the fire, cooking sausages and telling ghost stories!

The three-arched Summer House backs onto it. The striking white marble statue is by the Serbian sculptor Ivan Mestrovic of his wife.

# The Pleasure Grounds & Pond

The Bell Door leads out of the Walled Garden into the Pleasure Grounds between two stone sphinxes. In the early months of the year, spring flowers grow here in abundance. Wild orchid thrive on the sunny banks below the limes near the Pleasure Pond. Beside the pond is Cannock House, surrounded by patches of poor sandy soil where native wild heathers are encouraged. These are characteristic of the heath land native to this part of Sussex, and give a clear indication of how much of the park might look if it had not been grazed for centuries by the deer. Rich in insect life, grass is purposefully left long at times and on the lake, kingfishers and feral Mandarin ducks thrive.

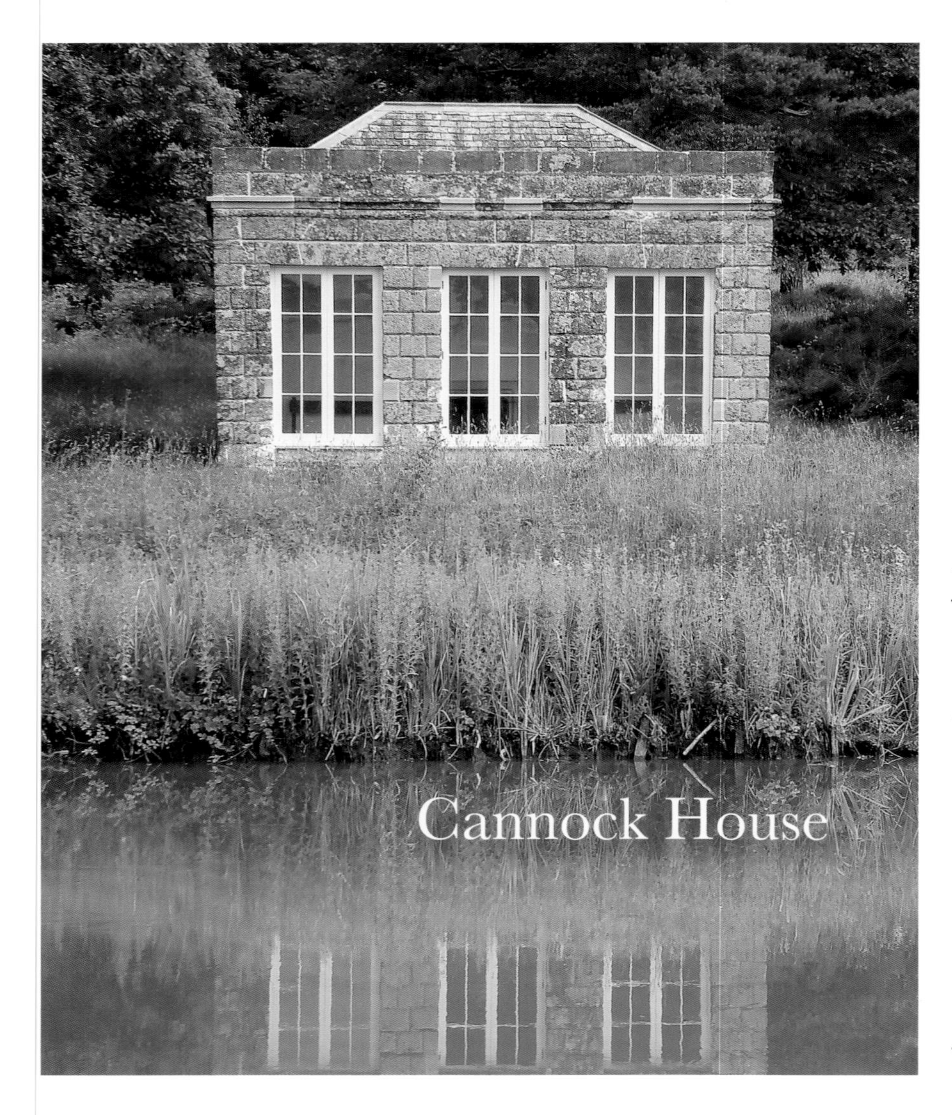

Cannock House

*Cannock House is constructed of local sandstone, similar to that used in Parham House and other buildings in the park. It is particularly friable, and a number of blocks have had to be replaced.*

*There are no records as to when it was built, but it probably dates from the late 18th or early 19th centuries, when Sir Cecil Bisshopp, the 8th Baronet, laid out the Pleasure Grounds.*

*The River God was brought to Parham by Robert Curzon from Hagley Hall, near Cannock Chase in Staffordshire, in the mid 19th century. The family gave him the nickname "Old Cannock", from which it is thought the Cannock House derives its name.*

*The building was probably used for picnics and for enjoying the views across the West Plain to the South Downs. In the 19th century it was also known as the "Fishing Temple".*

*In 1748, the mutilated body of a man called Hawkins was found in the pond, which at the time adjoined the public highway through the Park. He had been brutally murdered by a smuggler called Mills, who was eventually brought to justice and hanged in chains on nearby Slindon Common.*

# The River God

# Veronica's Maze

As you walk back towards the house, you will see the maze. Named after Veronica Tritton, it was built as part of the celebrations for the "Year of the Maze" in 1991. Made of brick and turf, its design is adapted from the 16th century embroidery on the Great Bed in the house. To reach the centre, you must go forward at all times. You may fork left or right when faced with a choice, but you may NOT turn left or right at a crossroads, nor turn back!

# Flower arranging

***Alicia Pearson started the tradition of flower arrangements all through the House for the enjoyment of visitors. The tradition is still maintained, and the flower arranging, done 'the Parham way', is undertaken by a dedicated team. Sometimes as many as thirty buckets of flowers and greenery are cut each week.***

Cricket has been played at Parham since 1898, when it was reported that "Lord Zouche gives his permission for the young men of Parham to play cricket in the park and it is much appreciated". Today the Club plays regularly in summer. Before 1950 the membership was exclusive to Parham estate workers, but today the players are drawn from a much wider area.

# Two Crickets in summer ...

*Photograph by Ted Benton*

***The rich variety of habitat at Parham provides a home to many interesting species of birds, animals and insects. The endangered Field Cricket was introduced under Natural England's Recovery Programme, and now the male cricket can be heard during May and June.***

*St Peter's Church, Parham*

***Recent archaeological investigations suggest that the earliest part of the church dates from c.1150. It was largely rebuilt in the early 1800s and seats nearly 80 people in the high box pews. On Christmas Day the fire in the family pew is lit.***

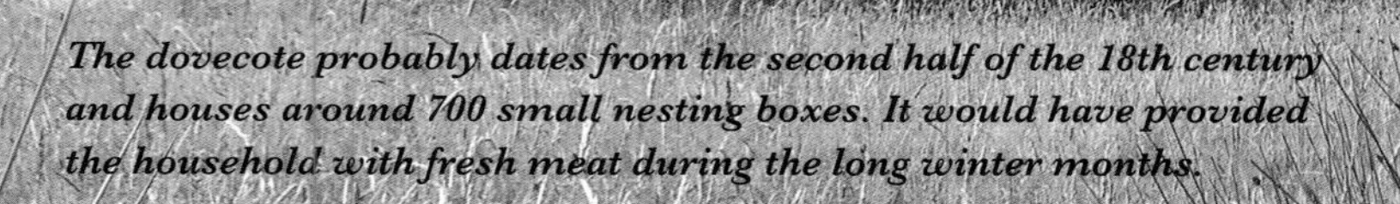

*The dovecote probably dates from the second half of the 18th century and houses around 700 small nesting boxes. It would have provided the household with fresh meat during the long winter months.*

# Veteran Trees

*(Right): Veteran oak tree; some of those surviving in the park are over 500 years old.Parham suffered badly in the Great Storm of 1987. An ongoing planting programme is being carried out to provide a new generation of oaks.*

*In 1669 it is recorded that Parham oak was being used by the Royal Navy. Ageing and damaged trees are allowed to decay naturally, providing a vital habitat for insects, funghi and bats. The Parham trees harbour one of the richest densities of lichens in south east England.*

*The park is a haven for wildlife. It has one of the largest heroneries in Sussex, dating back to the early 1830s.*

*Heron*

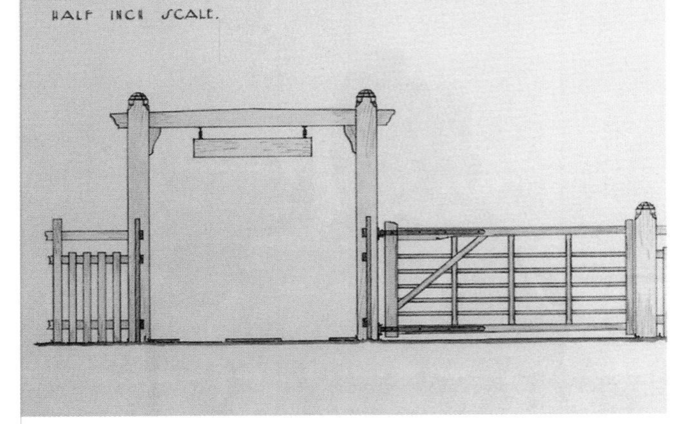


*Drawing for North Drive gates. Dated April 1936.*

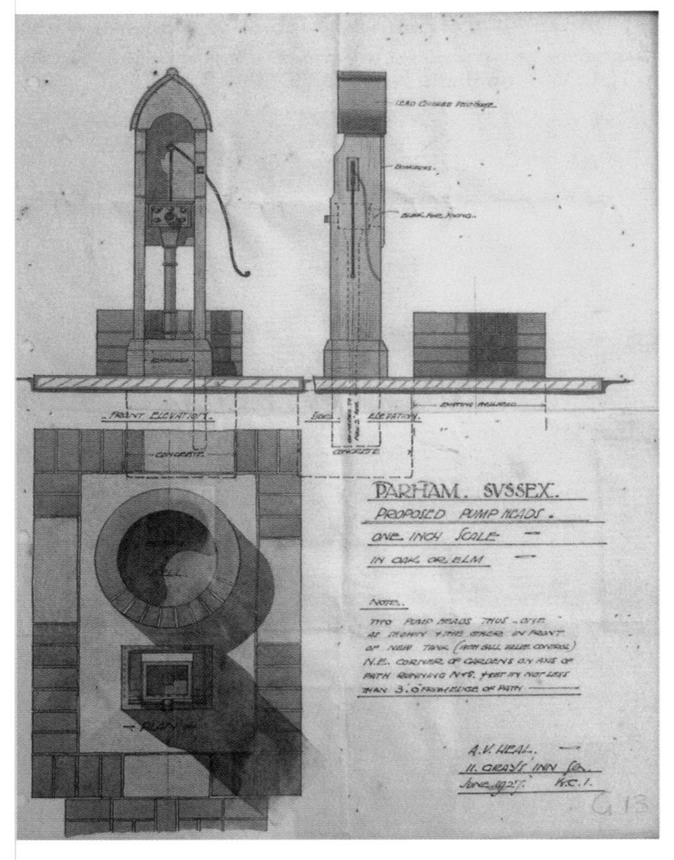


*Drawing by Victor Heal for garden pump heads. Dated June 1927.*